The Love of Your Life Is You:
A Step-by-Step Workbook to Loving Yourself

Copyright © 2021 Dushka Zapata

Second edition copyright © 2024

All rights reserved

ISBN: 979-8343082531

Cover design and illustrations by Dan Roam.

A few years ago I published a book titled "The Love of Your Life Is You." It is a workbook with step-by-step instructions on how to love yourself.

I wanted this book to feel so special in the reader's hands: printed on high quality paper and full of delightful color illustrations by Dan Roam.

Over time I got the feedback that this workbook was truly useful and needed a more accessible price point — so that people could get many copies for a book club, a group of friends, or a classroom.

So, I've finally reprinted the book. It's the same content, with black and white illustrations: "The Love of Your Life Is You, Unplugged" a second edition for anyone who wants to get a copy at a more affordable price.

Get this book with a lined notebook, make some tea and spend a quiet afternoon in the best possible company, with the love of your life: you.

*A guide to writing your book about
how to love yourself.
(Because, no one else can tell you how to do it)*

Contents

Introduction	1
What You'll Need.	2
But what does it mean, to love yourself?	4
Part 1: As I get to know myself, I develop faith in me.	8
Part 2: I am less driven by what my ego wants me to do.	56
Part 3: I am more comfortable in the moment.	114
A quick summary: Your cheat sheet.	152
What happens as you learn to love yourself?	158
Author's note	161
About the Illustrator	163
About the Author	165

Introduction

This is a workbook about how to love yourself.

What do I mean by "workbook"?

I mean it's not something you read, but something you write.

I can't tell you know to love yourself. I can tell you about my own process and hope you find it useful.

This is a guide, but it's not my book. It's your book.

You are going to write it.

What you'll need:

A sense of adventure.

Time to take breaks to think and feel.

A willingness to push through parts that are difficult or uncomfortable.

An ability to recognize when you need additional resources. This might be consulting with a doctor before trying a new diet or exercise regimen, or doing further research on anything that is not sufficiently clear or that you need to learn more about.

Alacrity, to question your own beliefs.

A lined or blank notebook you love.

Colored pens or pencils. (You don't really need colors, but they're fun.)

But what does it mean, to love yourself?

LOVING YOURSELF IS NOT SOMETHING YOU DO.
"THERE. ALL DONE."

LOVING YOURSELF IS A PRACTICE.
AGAIN. AGAIN. AGAIN.

Loving yourself is not something you do but something you practice, a series of interconnected actions that involve treating yourself like something special and wonderful.

You eat well and exercise and do things to assist you in the battles that you fight — for example, I have anxiety and do my best to go to yoga, breathe, get a good night of sleep. I work hard at defying my own thoughts. (We will cover all these things in detail later.)

You step away from things that hurt you — friends who put you down or the job that doesn't fulfill or inspire you or the person who, well, doesn't do what they say they're going to do.

You can do better, not because you can go find another person but because you have yourself.

You do things for you that you would do for someone you love — fun things like getting you those shoes you like and harder things like standing up for yourself, or following through on your own promises.

Following through on your own promises is extremely important because every time you do you teach yourself that you are someone you can count on.

"I can't go get drinks. I said I'd go to the gym four times a week and I skipped yesterday."

You do things that make you happy and let you get to know yourself and you become really involved in creating something. A pot of soup, a garden, a book. It doesn't matter what. It's yours and it's for you and maybe also supports and nourishes others.

You take ownership of everything that affects your vital space — you build sacred things like habits and ceremony and boundaries. You come to terms with disappointing others. You learn to say no.

You say yes a lot too and surprise yourself by making unexpected plans — yes, yes. Book the trip to Portugal. Get that beautiful painting so you can place it over your bed. Drink every day out of a beautiful handmade cup.

Do senseless things, less for goals and objectives and more for the sheer pleasure of it.

People who love themselves don't always. This is work. Loving yourself is like every other feeling — inconsistent, fluid, sometimes dismaying — but in the end you build a relationship with someone truly interesting you know you can count on.

Should we get started?

Signs I need to love myself more

I need external validation — it's how I define myself.

I constantly compare myself to others.

I feel lost and can't tell the difference between "we" and "me".

I put others down.

I change a lot depending on who I'm with.

I don't let others see me.

Being alone makes me uncomfortable.

I blame others.

A lot of the things I go through I seem to be going through again and again.

I take criticism really hard.

Navigating difficult emotions is almost intolerable.

I experience difficulty setting boundaries.

I assume that the way people act towards me is about me.

I make commitments towards myself and don't follow through.

I don't take care of myself.

I do unhealthy things that hurt me.

I talk to myself in ways I would never talk to anyone else.

I cannot trust others.

I'm never proud of me.

Let's improve upon all this.

Start Here

Do you believe self-care or putting yourself first is selfish?

Open your notebook.
Write the answer to this question.

Is this what you believe? Why?

_____
_____
_____
_____

Why is putting yourself first selfish?

_____
_____
_____
_____

What does being self-centered mean to you?

_____
_____
_____
_____

Write down a few examples of "selfish" behavior.

_____

_____

_____

_____

There are many meanings to the term "self-centered".

The first is independent, sovereign, self-reliant, not easily influenced by others.

The concept of loving yourself, caring for yourself, might be self-centered but is not selfish. It is designed for you to give yourself what you need so you can in turn give to others from a healthier, rather than depleting place.

If you are the boat others need to navigate choppy waters, what happens to everyone if the boat is not well maintained?

If you are a pitcher of water that quenches everyone's thirst, what happens to everyone if the pitcher is empty?

Loving yourself makes giving and caring for others possible.

Being self-centered can also refer to someone mostly interested in herself. This can lead to carelessness or intolerance. A self-centered person can be selfish: devoted to herself, to the exclusion of others instead of for others. That is not who we are. It's not what we are doing. It's not what this workbook is about.

Your sacred quest: Make your well-being a priority

I know. "You should make your well-being a priority" is an obvious statement.

But, what does it mean?

Write down what it means to you. You want to see if what you think now changes after you have read this section, so you will write what it means to you twice — here, and again at the end of this section.

_____

_____

_____

_____

If you set the alarm to get up and go for a run but you haven't been sleeping well, what is the right thing to do for your well-being? Go back to sleep or get out of bed and go for a run?

If you are struggling with anxiety, do you work through your feelings or look for a distraction? What is best for your well-being, time alone, or time with others?

If someone in your life holds a position of great importance but your relationship with them is toxic, do you cut them out of your life? What is best for your well-being? Your history with them, or distance from them?

Doing what's best for your well-being is really difficult. Sometimes, it's impossible to tell.

This is why we need silence. To hear ourselves sort out what it is that would truly be best for us.

Take some time to think about this and make a list of what would be good for you.

_____

_____

_____

_____

Notice how the answers can vary depending on the day.

How can you get better at finding the right answer?

_____

_____

_____

_____

(Only you can answer this question. No one else has access to the answer.)

This brings me to my next point, and explains why it's so important.

Learn to be at peace with silence.

How does being alone make you feel?

_____

_____

_____

_____

How can you learn to want more rather than less alone time?

_____

_____

_____

_____

How can you make time to be alone?

_____

_____

_____

_____

How can you protect this space only you can create for yourself?

_____

_____

_____

_____

In solitude I find silence, peace and an ability to sort myself out.

I don't sort myself out as a result of effort. It's like my brain needs the space to sort everything out without my active intervention.

After I have been alone for a few hours I come out feeling grounded, centered and with a calmer, more balanced perspective.

What I seek in solitude is me.

Three things helped me fall in love with being alone.

The first one was realizing what being alone gave me, and fully taking advantage of it.

I began to sleep in the middle of the bed. I used every pillow. I organized my things the way I wanted them. Kept only food I liked in the fridge

I get up in the middle of the night to write, have many bowls but no plates, many cups but no pots or pans.

I listen to the same song all day if I want to. I have a closet all to myself.

Being alone grants you a particular kind of space. Every day I learn how to occupy more of it.

The second thing was treating myself the way I would treat someone I was in love with. It requires that I be very tuned into what I want or need. (We will think about this a lot throughout this workbook.)

Dushka, look. I got you a book. I ran you a bath with special salts. Let's go out on a date with ourselves that includes a lot of wandering. Let's find and stock up on your favorite foods. I did some research on movies I thought you might like. Would you like me to make some popcorn?

The third thing has to do with creation. I'm a writer, so I write, but it can be anything. A scrapbook. A cake. A painting. An enormous multi-layered project that will require I leave art supplies scattered everywhere. What a mess. My mess.

Put a working bench in the middle of the living room. (Who needs a living room?) Put an easel in the dining room. (Who needs a dining room?)

Let what you create take over. If you are with what you make, you will never be alone.

What would being alone give you?

_____

_____

_____

_____

What do you long for, in that special place?

_____

_____

_____

_____

What things would you do to treat yourself?

_____

_____

_____

_____

What do you want to create?

_____

_____

_____

_____

This is a question we will come back to but start thinking about it and taking notes now.

Comparing yourself to others.

How often do you compare yourself to others?

_____

_____

_____

_____

Write down how it makes you feel.

_____

_____

_____

_____

Write down what it helps you accomplish.

_____

_____

_____

_____

How does comparing yourself to others contribute to your life?

_____

_____

_____

_____

The first time I went to a yoga class I did not want to go back.

Everyone was better than me.

Everyone was bendier and more graceful. I couldn't even touch my toes.

The more I looked at others the worse I did.

Not only because I felt increasingly inadequate but because I forced myself into the poses they could do and I couldn't.

Ouch.

I found that if I focused on myself I made a lot more progress.

I had to begin by accepting exactly where I was.

I had to determine what worked for me, regardless of what worked for everyone else.

I stopped comparing myself to others when I understood that every second spent looking at someone else would be better spent working on myself.

I practice resisting the temptation of comparing myself to others. My progress is my progress. My success is my success. My pain is my pain. My path is my own.

The measure of me is me.

The alternative is a perpetual sense of inadequacy, feeling like I'm flawed, like I can't, like I shouldn't, like I lack, like I'm deviant, irregular, out of line.

I really don't want this to be something I do to myself.

Can you identify when you compare yourself to others?

_____

_____

_____

_____

What would you like to be doing with that time and energy?

_____

_____

_____

_____

What are the things you want to work on instead?

_____

_____

_____

_____

Next time you compare yourself to someone, return to your list of things you want to work on and turn your attention to that instead.

Do it again and again.

Remember. This is a practice.

How do you talk to yourself?

Let's say I work with someone no one on my team believes in.

Ugh. We don't consider the work she does is ever good enough.

What a loser.

We find again and again that when something goes wrong, she is to blame.

The more time goes by the more we lose confidence in her. As a result, we give her fewer projects to lead and seldom ask for her opinion.

When we compare her to others, anyone else is better than her.

Honestly, her silence is best. It's better that she do nothing, rather than get everything wrong. We are tired of cleaning up after her.

How does this sound? Harsh, even cruel? Do you feel that it possibly lacks support, compassion?

Because, this is self-criticism. The team I am referring to is me. That woman who is never good enough is me.

I talk to myself in a way I would never treat another.

Oh my god you are not good enough. Again, this is your fault. Everyone is better than you. Don't speak up. Don't take risks.

I am the one keeping me down, afflicting my spirit, impacting my productivity.

This is exhausting. I am exhausting myself.

If you think self-criticism can motivate you or make you strong, think about that woman. Self criticism is isolating, diminishing.

It affects your perspective and your creativity. It drains you of energy and dries up your self-confidence.

It's so plain to see that woman on this make-believe team would respond better to assistance. To encouragement.

To the beam of light that is feeling someone believes in you.

You are good enough. It's OK to make mistakes. This is how you learn. This is how you practice.

Take a breath and try again. I'll be right here, rooting for you.

Hey, Dushka. You know what?

Berating myself has never resulted in me modifying my behavior.

Stop bad-mouthing you.

Make a list of things you typically tell yourself.

_____

_____

_____

_____

Does your inner voice criticize you, put you down?

Can you really work on something if your enemy is on the inside?

If you are talking to yourself in a way that you would never speak to someone else, practice. Practice replacing it with something you'd say to someone you love.

Alongside the list of things you tell yourself, add what you'd like to replace that with.

_____

_____

_____

_____

Learn to ask yourself what you need.

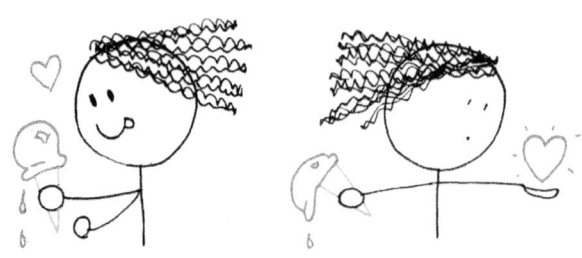

It sounds so easy, doesn't it? How is it possible you don't know what you need? But, you don't.

You see, most wants are misdirected.

I want ice cream because it's cold and creamy but really I want to be soothed because I'm nervous about where my life is going and ice cream is easier than figuring out what it is that I need to do to not be a cyclical catastrophe.

I want a big bowl of crunchy, salty things but really I'm just tired and what I want is to unwind and give my brain a break and feel like I have a place to set myself down.

I want clothes and shoes and shiny things but really my closet is already full and what I want is something that addresses this emptiness and absence of beauty.

I want a lover and a hotel room and an afternoon out of time but really what I want is to go back to when things were simpler and maybe to feel pleasure in the place of all this jagged loneliness and complexity.

My brain tells me she wants something because it's easier to want that than to identify — and quench — the want that is real.

Write it down.

What do you want?

_____

_____

_____

_____

Look under that. And under that. And under that.

What do you want?

_____

_____

_____

_____

Ask yourself this question over and over.

Know this question has no end (or the end is temporary.)

You will never know what you want.

If you do, it will be fleeting, because humans are constantly evolving and you are no exception. Every fix is temporary. It's not a cure. It's just a fix. You will need another one soon — so soon.

What you can do is stop regarding this as a problem and begin seeing it as an adventure.

Conceive of yourself as an explorer, a seeker, a wanderer, an experimenter.

Travel, within and outside of yourself.

CONCEIVE OF YOURSELF AS AN EXPLORER INSIDE YOURSELF.

Identify things that make you feel awake, alert, connected, curious — and do more of those.

Identify the things that make you feel like lead, like dread, dismay, and do less of those.

Get away, even if getting away feels counterintuitive. Even if what is making you feel this way is "what everybody does." Even if others — even others you trust — say you are making a mistake.

Recognize the things you don't do because you are afraid and learn to tell the difference between *"I am scared but that's a yes"* and *"that's a no."* This is very hard and even after years of practice one will mimic the other which means you have to be brave and also that you will make many mistakes.

Finally, recognize that what you seek is not resolved by a sudden awakening, a flash of insight, enlightenment, but rather a process that will test you, confuse you, perplex and frustrate you.

That right there — this process, disruptive, uncomfortable, painful as hell is where the marrow of life is. Not in the purpose that you are supposed to find.

Life is not in the answer. There is no answer. Life is in the desperate, frantic, often painful, sometimes astonishing search.

If that is what you are feeling — *"what the hell is this? What the hell is this?"* — you are doing something right.

Do you hear me?

You are doing it right.

Don't settle

You know what we do? We settle.

We find ourselves in a certain situation and convince ourselves this is what it has to be. *(I feel trapped in my relationship, I've gained twenty pounds, I don't like my job, I feel a constant state of anhedonia or ennui.)*

This is life. I can't change this.

No one is supposed to be happy all the time.

Never, ever believe mediocrity, low grade despair or bleh is what you have to live with. Things can always get better — even when they are good.

Identify what you should not have to be OK with, and devise small steps to get out.

Do something that inches you closer to your escape every day.

There is no limit to how happy you can be.

You just have to work at it.

Go ahead. Make a list of all the things you should not be OK with.

_____

_____

_____

_____

Beside each one, make a list of small steps to get out.

Plot your escape. No matter how trapped you think you are, plotting an escape is always possible.

Think about this sentence: there is no limit to how happy you can be. Are you ever suspicious of happiness? Worried that the other shoe is going to drop? That you will jinx things?

Write down all the times you limit your own happiness, thinking it's too much.

_____

_____

_____

_____

Then, think how illogical that actually is.

Finding versus exploring.
Finding versus creating.

In my experience, the process of loving yourself is less about "finding" (which implies something outside yourself) and more about inner exploration.

By this I mean it's a process, takes a long time, and has an evolution (meaning, it changes. You change).

I ask myself what I want and then am curious about what happens when I get it. (*Hmmm. I thought that was what I wanted but I guess not.*)

I look for the things that I like and that are important to me.

I identify the things that are not me and do less of them. (I understand cars are sexy but honestly. I could not possibly care any less what you drive.)

Sometimes this is hard because a lot of other people like certain things, so not liking them makes me feel like there is something wrong with me. (Nope. I'm OK.)

A few examples I can think of:

Being at a party and arriving home late and wondering why I feel so exhausted and so hollowed out. (I don't like parties.)

Being alone for many days at a time and wondering why I feel so empty. (I love social interaction — I just need time to recharge.)

Writing and feeling electric, plugged into the whole universe. (Yep. This is it. This is what I want more, more, more of.)

Falling in love and getting married and feeling like that ring felt like a noose. Marriage is wonderful. Just because something is wonderful doesn't mean it's right for me.

So that's what you do — step. Review. Step. How do I feel? Step. What do I need? Step. Why does this feel awful when it's supposed to feel wonderful?

This exploration requires time alone so that you can hear yourself over the voices of others. It's not tiresome or stressful (well, OK. Sometimes it is.). But mostly it's the delightful discovery of this interesting person that you are.

You get to know her, and slowly, astonishingly, you find who you are.

Make lists. Make lists of everything you just read.

What do you want?

_____

_____

_____

_____

How does it change?

_____

_____

_____

_____

How can you regard it as an adventure rather than something frustrating?

_____

_____

_____

_____

How do you change?

_____

_____

_____

_____

Learn to meditate.

It's easy for me to believe that improvement, perfection and happiness are somewhere else. As soon as I find someone to share my life with. As soon as I land the right job. As soon as I lose five more pounds.

This moving, running, always grasping for something just beyond my reach is exhausting.

Meditation is a rest from that. It's sitting with everything that is.

You, wild and imperfect. You, uncomfortable and scared. You, twitchy and overwhelmed with all the thoughts you can't stop thinking.

Just sit. Just breathe. Not to feel better, not to get better, not to overcome.

It's just about paying attention. That's it.

Meditation will change your life.

If you give it a chance you will feel calmer, more focused and happier.

Meditation makes you emotionally stronger because instead of getting "hooked into" the feelings that you experience, you recognize them as something separate from who you are.

It's harder for them to take you on that wild, unsustainable, exhausting roller coaster ride.

What you need to do to be an accomplished meditator is to focus on your breath.

That's it.

Do it every day, even if you only focus on your breath for a couple of minutes.

Pick a quiet spot and time of day. You can, for example, wake up a bit earlier than everyone else.

Or, pick any time of day and hide in the bathroom.

You need to be, just for a snippet of time you lovingly give yourself, free of external distractions.

Make sure you sit in a position where your spine is straight.

Your mind will do what minds do. It will think. It will wander. It will produce list after list of things to do, things you need to get at the supermarket, things you have forgotten, things you better not have forgotten, a list of more important things to do than sit there and do nothing.

It will tell you that it's much more important to be busy.

It will make your nose itch.

It will tell you you are sooooo soooo sleeeeepy.

It will tell you to be very concerned that you are not doing it right.

It will get you to freak out.

Allow all this to happen. Regard it without judgement. *"Huh. Look! All the things Dushka said!"*

Ignore everything, let it pass you by, and focus on your breath.

Welcome to the very best thing you can do for yourself, your life, your sanity and your happiness.

Keep your special notebook by you when you meditate.

When you are done, write.

See what you came up with when your mind was quiet.

_____

_____

_____

_____

Habits, rituals and a practice.

A habit is an activity you have repeated so many times that your brain switches to automatic. You don't have to think. You don't do it because you want to. You don't even question it.

Our life is a system of habits that are all interconnected. Changing one can (and often does) affect the others.

Changing your habits is a certain way to change your life but it's hard to do because most of them have faded into the fabric of your days and have become invisible. You can't change what you can't see.

A ritual is the opposite of a habit. It requires your full presence and attention and as such it wakes up your brain.

There is something sacred in a ritual. Its meaning is bigger than the immediate action you are taking. Connection. Community. Awareness. Devotion.

Let's look at these one at a time.

What is a habit?

This is such a critical question because a lot of things I have attributed to my character (such as *"I am a worrier"*) are really just habits, habits that I have spent my entire life inadvertently reinforcing.

Some examples are always picturing the worst case scenario (I think that it "prepares me" but really it just stresses me) or repeating to myself things likely to discourage me (I'm so bad at that).

What are habits you have that would like to change? (Examples: codependency, jealousy, possessiveness.)

What are some habits that you've picked up along the way that you intentionally reinforce and work on?

_____

_____

_____

_____

What habits are you practicing?

_____

_____

_____

_____

Here are the ones I am practicing. If you like them, you can practice them too.

To assume others have good intentions and are trying their best. It's better to travel through life unburdened by suspicion, better to be disappointed sometimes than to be encumbered always.

To banish blame. I prefer to be accountable for who I am and what I do. I prefer to be powerful.

To imagine the best-case scenario instead of the worst-case scenario. They are equally plausible and when the worst does happen it only hurts one time, instead of the recurring blows inherent in fervent anticipation.

To interpret the story of my life in a way that casts me as fortunate.

To learn to ignore my inner voice any time it tells me I can't do something. The world imposes enough limits on me. I don't need to contribute against myself.

To remember that the difference between an adventure (exciting) and an obstacle (frustrating) is how I choose to regard it.

To identify what I don't like within me and dedicate all the resources available to me to address them.

To love and admire the people closest to me. We become so much of what we surround ourselves with.

To find cruelty unacceptable.

If a series of conclusions can all be equally true, I can choose the option that makes me suffer the least. To suggest to myself that *"life is meaningless"* or that *"he never really loved me"* is needlessly painful.

To believe in luck, in miracles and in magic. To believe in absurdly frequent serendipity. To believe that anything can happen.

To see that I am always learning something new.

To question what I believe in.

Now, you.

What are your deliberate habits?

_____

_____

_____

_____

What life do you want to create?

_____

_____

_____

_____

Rituals

A ritual is the act of taking something I already do for myself and adding a few deliberate ingredients: a pause, attention, full presence, an intention, involving more of my senses.

This makes a necessary everyday routine something more sacred, something that protects me from taking for granted all the every day things that make my life more fortunate and beautiful.

Create very simple rituals. Any time, about anything.

A bath with bath salts. A peaceful dinner. An evening meditation.

I like morning rituals.

I get up early so I have quiet time for myself.

I make coffee or tea.

I take a few long, slow deep breaths.

I stretch.

I spend 10 minutes meditating.

I set an intention for the day.

I ask myself one question: what do I need? I think about the answer and try to go deeper than anything obvious.

I wrap up by noting something that corresponds to each one of my senses: what do I see? What can I touch? What can I smell? What do I taste? What can I hear?

To me, starting the day like this is so much better than allowing myself to be engulfed by my email, or letting the day rush towards me full force. This way, I set the tone for the cadence of my day.

Write down a ritual you'd like to create.

_____

_____

_____

_____

Make it a part of your life.

Practice.

Practice is revolutionary.

It is the most underestimated, most powerful tool available to us.

It's the door to understanding something. To learning something. To getting good at something. To getting better at something.

It's the way to accomplish something I never thought I could.

It's how something I previously thought impossible one day becomes easy.

But most of all, practice is where you meet yourself.

Let's say I want to become a good writer. What will it take?

Practice. To be a good writer, I need to write.

Let's say I'm going to practice from Monday to Sunday, every day.

If I start on Monday, will I be slightly better by Friday?

Not necessarily.

Monday might be rusty. Tuesday might be smoother. Wednesday, catastrophic. Thursday I want to give up and never practice again.

This isn't working. Why did I think this was a good idea?

Friday is frustrating and difficult.

Saturday is smooth.

Sunday is —

What a waste.

The lesson here is not in getting better or worse but in how I meet my bad days and my good days.

Do I get exasperated? Do I give up? Do I run?

I want to run.

Can I learn to meet my bad days with equanimity, to have bad days not matter so that my emotions remain stable while my skill does what it will?

Practice cannot be about right or wrong.

It's about showing up, accepting where I am at and realizing that if I consider it similar to repetition, if I consider it tedious, I am missing the point.

It's a gift: something I can count on forever.

It will always be there waiting for me.

Even if I get everything wrong a thousand times I can always, always begin again.

What do you want to get good at?

_____

_____

_____

_____

What is it that you want to adopt, see as an integral part of your life?

_____

_____

_____

_____

Where would you like to find the magic of always being able to start over?

_____

_____

_____

_____

Discipline

LACK OF DISCIPLINE.

What is the point of being disciplined?

The point of being extremely disciplined is everything.

A lack of discipline is you, scattered, dispersed, disorganized, prey to all the things that contribute to nothing ever getting done: procrastination, laziness, indecision and an absence of drive.

Why don't I feel motivated? Where can I find that hunger? How do I accomplish what I dream of doing? Why is everything so difficult?

I want that, but it's unattainable. That's impossible.

Discipline is you, focused, set free from all those things inside of you that hold you back.

DISCIPLINE IS YOU, <u>FOCUSED</u>, SET FREE FROM ALL THOSE THINGS THAT HOLD YOU BACK.

Action begets motivation. With discipline, a life of leaving everything for tomorrow, a life of frustrating, sporadic effort, becomes structured, stable, directed, inspired.

Discipline means you turn down instant gratification (pass the cookie) in favor of something more significant that you get later.

It's how you decide to follow through, and how you get to an objective — often one that once seemed it couldn't be done.

Discipline teaches you to persevere, to endure, to not give up, to resist temptation.

It teaches you about self-control.

Discipline is a mark — and a way to develop — character.

It's with discipline that you follow through on what you say you are going to do. This is how you prove to yourself that you can do something — as such, discipline is also the key to develop confidence and self-esteem.

If you ever wonder how to be successful, how it is that people bridge who they are now to who they want to be, the answer is discipline.

You can start small.

What are the promises you want to make for yourself?

Make them easy but make sure you follow through.

Keeping the promises you make to yourself is directly related to self-esteem. They are proof you can count on you.

Some examples: drink more water. Walk 10 minutes a day. Meditate.

If one day you don't do it, scramble back on as soon as you can (later that day, for example).

_____

_____

_____

_____

Remember: discipline allows for missteps. Don't spend time beating yourself up. Get right back onto what you promised yourself you would do

Learn to question your thoughts.

Have you heard about Byron Katie?

She's a modern day Socrates.

She discovered, consistent with the ancient Greeks, Zen tradition and Buddhism, that believing her own thoughts was the source of all her suffering.

She proceeded to write several best-selling books based on this insight and developed a method called "The Work."

The intent of "The Work" is for the thoughts that you are convinced are true to loosen their hold on you.

She doesn't want you convinced they are not true.

She wants you to wonder.

Here is a quick summary of "The Work".

Identify something you are convinced of that makes you suffer.

This could be anything: *I am not good enough, no one will ever love me, I am a loser.*

For the purposes of this demonstration of "The Work" let's go with:

My boss thinks my work sucks.

You then ask yourself the following questions that you need to really, deeply ponder for a while, not check off in quick succession.

In other words, sit there and really search inside yourself.

Is this true? (A typical response would sound like *Oh my god yes my boss thinks everything I do is crap just this morning he glared at me and said….*)

Can I absolutely know it's true? (*Well yes I just told you this is what I believe in!*)

How do I react — what happens — when I believe this? (*It's so stressful it makes me feel sad and small and like nothing I do is ever good enough! Ack! Ack!*)

Who would I be without this thought? (*I feel…free. Peaceful.*)

Once you are done with all the questions comes the best part.

The turnaround.

Turn your thought around by considering different versions of the exact opposite.

To continue with my example, the turnarounds could be:

My boss loves me.

I think I suck.

I think my boss sucks.

Take each one of your masterfully created turnarounds and add "The Work" again. (Is this true? Is this truer?)

What happens to your brain when you do this and sleep on it is incredible.

"The Work" done diligently implants in your mind new possibilities, other alternatives to things that cause you anxiety, and sets you free.

What are some things you believe that make you suffer?

Examples: No one will ever love me. Nobody understands me.

Write them down.

_____

_____

_____

_____

Can you put these beliefs through "The Work"? It's really hard, but they really change your brain.

Learn to recognize your stories.

LEARN TO RECOGNIZE YOUR STORIES.

NOPE.

"NOT GOOD ENOUGH."
"THEY DON'T CARE."
"HE'S NOT INTERESTED."

YOU'RE JUST STORIES!!

I walk into a yoga class and feel so stiff. I have not done yoga for several days. I worry this class is going to be difficult, that I am not going to enjoy it.

I feel stiff. That's a fact. The rest is just a story.

My co-worker is acting aloof. *Is it me? Did I do something to offend him? Is he mad at me?*

It's true my co-worker is aloof. The rest is just a story.

I text someone and he doesn't text back. I spin out. *Why isn't he texting? Does he not care? Does he not want me? Is he not interested? Is he with someone else? Why is this happening to me?*

It's true he is not texting me. The rest is just a story.

Be aware of the things that are fact and the things that you add. Whatever it is that you are adding is just a story.

I know that sometimes the suffering is in the thing, but mostly, it's in the stories.

Is something causing you stress, anxiety?

Write it down.

_____

_____

_____

_____

Look at it.

Fact, or story?

At first, it will be difficult for you to tell the difference.

After a while, you will think "Story!" and suffer a whole lot less.

Then you get bad at recognizing stories again.

You return to practicing.

The worst case scenario

I spend so much time and so much energy fabricating catastrophes.

Let's think, Dushka. What is the worst that could happen?

But, wait.

What if?

What if this works out? What if you don't disappoint me, or if when you do we identify it as my (unreasonable) expectation and not your shortcoming?

And, what if you are real? What if we are real?

What if we stay?

What if there is always a park with a corner we can sit in, always a neighborhood to explore? What if we always find a quiet corner table at a delicious restaurant, waiting for us? What if we can always steal away a weekday afternoon?

What if this continues to grow, becomes all the things it can, stunning us with its awe and its beauty?

What if novelty and wonder never fade, wind their way into completely different ways to feel novelty and wonder?

What if the worst that could possibly happen is just me squandering this very perfect right now by spinning out on all the things that might quite possibly never go wrong?

I get to decide day by day, hour by hour, if I step into the fear or if I step into the faith. Our stories need us to believe in them.

What are your worst case scenarios? Write down your top five.

_____

_____

_____

_____

What is the best that could happen? Challenge each worst case scenario.

_____

_____

_____

_____

Alongside every worst case construct, write down the best.

Get crazy with it. Write down wondrous things that you consider irrationally positive.

Do this again and again.

Learn to recognize your ego.

Your ego is how you see yourself. A voice inside you that will contribute to you feeling stressed, anxious and inadequate. She (or he) will always steer you wrong. This is why it's important you learn to recognize it.

My ego is persuasive, high-strung, kinetic, hyperactive and indivisible from me. She wants me to believe I'm the center of the world, and wants to keep me safe.

She loves drama (closed, fabricated, theatrical) and despises risk (open, adventurous, uncomfortable).

Whenever I judge other people, the things they do, the choices they make, that's my ego trying to reassure me that whatever I am doing is much better.

Whenever I compare myself to others or insist on being right or get defensive or cast blame, that's her. Being perceived as fallible makes her frantic.

Whenever I repeat old patterns, that's her pulling me back in — she identifies "familiar" with safe so wants me to relive the same painful dynamics. She already knows it hurts but in its repetition has confirmed it's unlikely to kill me.

Whenever I'm more agitated about the story (not real) than about the fact (real), that's her. (Have you ever gotten angry over an argument that has only taken place in your head?)

Whenever I focus on approval or validation more than on what I want, that's her.

The way she relates to others is taking everything personally (because, it's all about her). This sounds like "you would if you loved me" or "you need to make me happy" or "I can fix you" or "please don't leave me". (*But Dushka. What if in leaving, you are being set free?*)

She believes that she needs to do something — be useful, be good — to deserve love.

The way she relates to creation or creativity or anything I do that might be beautiful is to sound like "I have no idea what I'm doing" or "I'm not doing it right" or "I failed". (*But, Dushka. What if you learned?*)

What you need to do with the ego is observe her. *Oh, wow. There you go again.* Question her. *Really? Is this story you just spun really truly true?* And soothe her. *Oh, my sweet. it's OK. We're going to be ok.*

Find your own ego. When does she (or he) emerge?

To help recognize her (or him): an out of control ego must be an expert at everything, does not accept ever being wrong, shows off, needs to be the best, is convinced the problem is everybody else, finds it difficult to apologize, regards everything as a competition and has to win.

_____

_____

_____

_____

A person with healthy self-esteem is happy to learn from others, sees herself clearly and does not link being right or winning with her self-worth.

The relationship between ego and self-esteem is inversely proportional. As such, anyone with a high ego has low self-esteem.

To further help you recognize your ego, here are some declarations that come from the ego:

Yas approval! What do we need to do to get more?

I want a promotion.

Others need to respect me. You need to respect me. Why doesn't anybody respect me?

Let's just obsess about this same thing and think about it over and over. Let's just not ever let it go.

I can't do that. Because, what are people going to think?

You really need to buy the most expensive of everything to show our formidable status.

That thing that just happened is proof that I am not superior to others and therefore I will not accept it.

Clearly I am not The Special One and as such I cannot support that decision.

I will never forgive you.

I suck. My life means nothing. I am not good enough.

I am anxious. So anxious.

I am afraid.

I need to be right.

I need to win.

I need to crush it. Crush you. Crush us. Crush this.

I am obsessed with how angry I am.

How hurt I am.

How disappointed I am.

Mine. That is mine. Everything is mine.

I am going to gossip and put down others to make myself feel like I'm better.

I am going to constantly compare myself to everyone.

I feel envy and jealousy all the time because everyone has a better life than me and is better than me and prettier than me and has more than me.

There isn't enough for everyone and I want it all for me.

I hate to lose. I will sulk. I will mope. I will moan.

Things didn't go well for me which means this is obviously somebody else's fault.

Nobody understands me.

As I am able to separate myself from my ego, my ego begins to make less decisions for me.

I begin to notice and shift my patterns.

I don't need to convince anyone about anything.

I realize that how people behave is a reflection of them, not a reflection of me. (This means that what someone else does cannot be the measure of my worth.)

Being misunderstood no longer makes me feel like I am alone.

I realize I cannot control, save, fix, improve or change anyone but me. This is liberating.

I get better at setting boundaries. Taking care of myself has become more important than compromising myself in an attempt to manage how you feel about me.

I seldom feel resentful since resentment feels like I am angry at someone else but is instead a sign that I have disrespected my boundaries.

I begin looking beyond the labels I typically use to define myself. (Yah I may be an introvert but I'm also quite social so maybe we are more than one thing?)

Can you recognize your ego?

Write down some examples of when he or she has driven you to misjudge a situation or make the wrong decisions.

_____

_____

_____

_____

Things that aren't good for you.

*Identify everything that you know is not good for you.
Everything.*

Habits. Patterns. People. Behavior.

_____

_____

_____

_____

Look at your notes. What are you inadvertently practicing, that you need to undo?

Write it all down here.

_____

_____

_____

_____

How can you make all these things smaller?

How can you spend less time, energy, resources on these things, and more on what is good for you?

_____

_____

_____

_____

Don't carry things that weigh you down. Are you feeling bitterness, anger, resentment, a drive for revenge? These things are the same as trying to get through a desert carrying poison instead of water. Throw it out. Let it go. Put it down. Forgive.

Don't spend any time with people who are not good for you. Is there anyone in your life constantly putting you down? Anyone you feel is toxic? Is anyone draining your energy? Do you have "frenemies" and can't explain why? You are fully responsible for the people you surround yourself with.

To help you identify what goes on this list, let's take a look at things we take on that we should have never taken on.

Let's begin with "making" someone love us.

When I understood what I am about to tell you I felt I had been shot with a truth bullet.

Here it is: The best things in life happen without my intervention.

I don't need to do anything to be loved. I am loved because I am me and this requires neither action nor effort.

I don't need to be on my toes for someone not to cheat on me. I don't need to take care of him or keep him under constant surveillance.

Loyalty is the default and cheating the anomaly.

Betrayal is not supposed to happen and I don't need to do anything to ensure that this remains the case.

I don't have to convince, persuade or chase anyone or win anyone over to get or catch either a good friend or a significant other.

Love — in any iteration — is like gravity. I don't do anything to keep my feet firmly planted on the ground.

These things are so true that if I instead decide to act — to exert effort, to work at it, to aggressively pursue, to supervise everything — I attract unhealthy relationships and wonder where to cast the blame.

I walk away from any dynamic that requires me to compromise my peace of mind. I do less. A lot less. I do nothing and witness an upside down life right itself.

What are the things you do to get someone to love you?

Who are the people you spend time chasing, who are not as interested in you as you are in them?

Write all this down. Think about what action to take.

_____

_____

_____

_____

Next. Let's take a look at another place we expend a lot of energy that goes nowhere.

I cannot and should not manage what other people think of me.

If I sit in silence and notice all the times I try in any way to manage what others think of me, I am shocked at the vast amounts of effort I expend in this futile endeavor.

This desperate, dank place is where poor boundaries come from, where people pleasing thrives, where we lose track of who we are and what we want in order to make an impression on people we don't even care that much about.

Who are these people, anyway?

If I set that down, I am free to spend all that effort and that energy on me. Me, who I am, what I want, how I want to live and who I want to surround myself with.

Go get it back. Get back this effort. Recover this energy. Set yourself free.

Make a list of the things you do in an effort to get others to think highly of you.

Anything you do to manage what others think or say about you.

_____

_____

_____

_____

Think about what to do about it.

Let's talk about how we lose ourselves in others.

Let's say I meet a guy.

I like him a lot so I pretend to like what he likes.

I want decisions to be easy so I go along with whatever he wants to do.

Soon I can't tell if I like something or "we" like something.

This is how I delude myself into thinking I have lost myself.

The truth is I don't actually lose myself (although it feels that way). I am still here, my voice making itself heard in unsuspecting ways.

I get angry at small things, feel irritable and impatient, resentful.

I begin to speak up. It's a voice of dissent and this confuses the guy. All he has ever known is me agreeing with everything so I can't fault him for suddenly not recognizing me.

I have never let him see me.

Speaking up feels good. It feels right. I do it in small ways first, and as my voice grows stronger I speak up in more meaningful ways.

I'm afraid, of course. Of losing his approval, of this guy deciding maybe we don't have that much in common and that he doesn't like me anymore.

But I've had enough of compromising myself and decide to push through this fear.

As hard as this choice is I'd rather not be liked by him than not be liked by me.

I don't want to go back to feeling lost, so empty and confused; not remembering what it's like to stand up for who I am.

And that's how you find yourself.

Write down the times you compromise yourself to be liked, to get approval.

_____

_____

_____

_____

Notice all the times you don't represent yourself, you don't let others see you, you betray yourself to be someone others want to be with.

Here is a quick look at things you are not responsible for. (No one is.)

If you do any of these things, you can stop.

> *Below each one of the sentences at the top of the next few pages, write down examples of you doing the very things you are not responsible for.*
>
> *How does stopping make you feel?*
>
> *How can you work towards not doing these things anymore?*

Here we go. I am leaving space for you to write your own examples below each one.

You are not responsible for keeping the peace or making sure others are getting along.

You are not responsible for another person's expectations of you.

You are not responsible for what another person thinks about you.

You are not responsible for explaining yourself.

You are not responsible for how another person behaves.

You are not responsible for getting someone to love you (or even like you).

You are not responsible for helping, rescuing or saving anyone other than yourself.

You are not responsible for anyone's happiness (or their emotional state).

You are not responsible for how your boundaries make another person feel.

You are not responsible for being anyone another person wants you to be.

Have uncomfortable conversations.

Make a list of uncomfortable conversations you should be having.

_____

_____

_____

_____

Why have you not had them?

_____

_____

_____

_____

How does leaving them for later make you feel?

_____

_____

_____

_____

Think about slowly checking off your list some of these conversations.

If something makes me uncomfortable I bring it up as soon as I clearly identify it. Keeping uncomfortable things to myself only succeeds in making me uncomfortable for longer.

I try to clearly, briefly state what makes me uncomfortable and then I stop.

I've noticed that when I'm talking about something difficult I chatter to fill the silence, unintentionally turning the conversation into a monologue.

Conversation takes at least two people and for that I need to contain my river of words.

I remind myself that discomfort is a feeling, not a fact. This means that I am dealing with a perception, not a truth. As such, I cannot be either right or wrong.

Trying to win the argument will create tension and make the other person feel not listened to.

Victory inflicts wounds on my relationships. I've learned that the price of winning arguments is not worth it. I would much rather understand, and be understood.

Along this same subject, have you noticed how we allow ourselves to be paralyzed by "awkward"?

Write down everything you avoid doing because it might be awkward.

_____

_____

_____

_____

Let's talk about what "awkward" is taking away from us.

Defying "awkward".

I bought into the notion that "awkward" was a big deal and that I needed to avoid it at all costs.

I weighed myself down with a secret for years lest things get "awkward".

I avoided repairing a valuable relationship because approaching the other person would have been awkward.

I disposed of treasured people to circumvent the awkward stage of navigating whatever needed to be navigated — a transition, a breakup, a change.

Please, accept awkward. Let things be awkward.
Embrace awkward.

Consider for a moment the cost (transitory awkwardness) versus what you stand to gain.

In the grand scheme of things, yeah, awkward is graceless and floundering and uncomfortable, but really, it's nothing compared to what is waiting on the other side.

Treat yourself as you would someone you love.

Parents don't know what they are doing.

This is not because they are incompetent. It's because they are human. Even when they love us madly and are doing their best they mess us up.

We grow up scarred from all the times we didn't get what we needed.

And one day we become adults.

There is power in being an adult. I am no longer small or helpless or defenseless.

Whatever it is I feel I did not get as a child, I can now get for myself.

By this, I don't mean just permission to get ice cream any time I want (although, ya! I definitely grant myself permission to get ice cream any time I want).

I mostly mean getting my most primal, most fundamental needs met, all the time, by me.

Dushka. I see you. I am listening.

I believe you.

It means I learn how to calm myself when I'm stressed, anxious or afraid. It means that when I'm in the grip of strong emotions I can give myself the chance to feel them (no more *"Dushka please don't be so emotional."*). It means I can set and hold boundaries. It means I can take care of myself.

This might mean making sure I'm getting enough sleep. It might mean deciding I don't need to "earn" the right to rest. It might mean keeping track of all the things that make me happy so I can have more of those things in my life.

The best thing I've done for myself in an effort to get me what I need is make room in my life to create: carving out time to write every day.

Anything you do to stand up for the kid you used to be (and still are, since the "adult" part is just a disguise) is incredibly healing, and it's called "reparenting". I can't recommend it enough.

Make a list of everything you want.

_____

_____

_____

_____

To be given permission to do something wonderful.

To buy something delightful for yourself (that you would never get for you, but do get for others. What is that about?).

To feel loved.

To feel cared for.

To feel safe.

You know who can give you all these things? You can.

Write out how you are going to do that, even if it takes the rest of your life.

_____

_____

_____

_____

Give yourself delicious food.

Food is delicious. It is nourishing. It is comforting. We associate it with sustenance, with support, with reassurance, with safety, with happiness, with pleasure, with luxury, with abundance, with relief, with encouragement. Look at all the roles it plays.

Diet is deprivation — not just from food but from all the things it represents.

How can I give myself more rather than less? More healthy, crunchy, fresh, delicious things. More colors on my plate. More variety. Give yourself delicious food. Don't punish yourself. In particular don't punish yourself with things that are not good for you, with things that don't make you feel wonderful.

Write about your relationship with food. What does it mean to you?

_____

_____

_____

_____

What would you feed someone you love? A friend, a child?

_____

_____

_____

_____

How can food be a way you show you you love you?

_____

_____

_____

_____

What does "eating healthy" mean to you?

_____

_____

_____

_____

*Do you need to explore this aspect of your life further?
Write down what you plan to do about that.*

_____

_____

_____

_____

Sleep

If I am well rested, I navigate the day with so much less friction. I ignore small difficulties, focus on what matters, have no difficulty making decisions, feel clear headed, do good work, exercise with vigor.

If I had a bad night small things are frustrating and feel insurmountable. *Nothing works. Nobody understands me. I can't think. I can't decide. Shhhh. Your breathing. It's so loud.*

To fix something, solve something, reduce anxiety, improve your relationships, to feel better, the place to start is sleep. Go to sleep.

Things that help me:

A dark room

No blue light — no screens, devices or television

Quiet, or a sound machine with sounds of nature

Aromatherapy

A comfortable mattress

A cool room

Going to bed at the same time every night, and not too early to avoid waking up in the middle of the night

No caffeine after 2:00 pm

A sleep story (to avoid obsessive, stressful thoughts)

Write down everything you can about how you sleep.

_____

_____

_____

_____

Notice when you sleep well and when you don't.

Spend time and effort finding a way for you to sleep better.

Sleeping better and my activity around giving myself a chance to rest has become one of my favorite rituals.

Your breath

Have you ever stopped to think about your breath? Have you taken the time to feel it, be conscious of it, notice it?

Did you know your breath is the tool we are given to regulate our system, our emotions?

Get to know your breath. Learn to take deep breaths, in through your nose, out through your mouth, and learn about the many different breathing techniques that help you self-regulate.

Exercise

This point is so much more important than looking good (although I think looking good is really important).

If you feel lost, like you don't know what to do with your life, like you have no idea what to do next, step one is to decide you are going to get in the best shape you have ever been in — the best shape for you.

Get up. Go on a run, or a walk, or a stretch. Join a gym, or a group. Just go.

In parallel, talk to a doctor. Do your research. How will you change your diet? What will you do for exercise? At what time? What works best for you?

In a life that feels rudderless, aimless, maybe even pointless, this alone will get you out of bed. It will give you structure, order and clear goals to move towards.

You will feel better as you get healthier. You will feel less blue, more motivated, more encouraged. You were designed to move.

As you get into your body you will tune into what you have been trying to tell you that you have been drowning out.

You will gain confidence as you begin to see the very real power you have to put yourself in a better place.

As one thing falls into place, other things will follow.

This is not easy. This is not instant. It's not magic. It's not linear. But it's real.

When you are lost, all you need is one small thing, an inkling, a hint, an intimation.

So, here. I will give it to you: it's your body.

What are some promises you can make to yourself around exercise?

_____

_____

_____

_____

How can you begin, round out, improve on whatever you are currently doing?

_____

_____

_____

_____

How does what you eat impact your workouts?

_____

_____

_____

_____

Can you get help? You can hire someone (such as a personal trainer) but also you have a whole world wide web of resources available to you.

Write all this down. Deliver on the promises you make to you.

Pleasure and your senses.

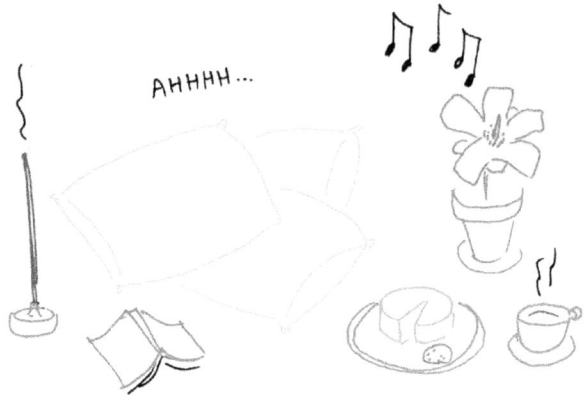

Does something make you feel dread? Trapped, resentful, apprehensive, dismayed, small, trepidatious?

Write it down. Look at it. Do less of whatever it is that makes you feel that.

_____

_____

_____

_____

Does something make you feel amazing, joyful, delicious, giddy, delighted, expansive, sunny, transported?

Pay attention. Write it down. Find more of that.

_____

_____

_____

_____

Pleasure is a compass. Let it guide you. That's what it's for.

Put some thought into your space.

Imagine a place. Your place. What if the love of your life was going to come live with you here? What would you do to design it, decorate it, prepare it?

Sit in a quiet space and think about your senses.
Sight, smell, touch, taste, sound.
How can your personal space appeal to each one of your senses?

Sight. What are your favorite colors? What do you want to look at? What have you recently seen that fills your eyes? This can be anything — sculpture, photographs, plants. Plants are wonderful because they appeal to so many of my senses.

Smell. What smells good? This can be incense, essential oils, even something you prepare in the kitchen; or plants that have a particular fragrance, like eucalyptus branches or lavender.

Touch. What feels good against your skin? Think about blankets, cushions, places to sit. Think about sheets and pillows. Think about a rug.

Taste. What food do you like? What tastes good and nourishing and comforting? Stock your kitchen thoughtfully.

Sound. What do you like to hear? What music do you want playing in this special place? And, where can you sit in silence?

Think about your brain. What does she (or he) like to learn? What does she like to read? What books can you get for her?

Divorce yourself from the notion that working on this special place has to be expensive. And, abandon the notion that you are in a hurry.

This special place will take a long time to get just right and it will always be changing, evolving, just like you, so in a sense you will never be done.

Explore websites. Look at a lot of images related to interior design. Notice what attracts you and how it makes you feel.

Peaceful? Inspired? Excited? Make notes. Take pictures. Follow hashtags.

Support local artisans and artists. Favor things made with care and by hand. Visit thrift stores and street markets. Get meaningful things from family and friends so that they are represented in your special place. Buy a handmade cup from your favorite tea house.

Get rid of anything that means nothing to you, or that isn't useful or beautiful. If this overwhelms you, do it slowly, drawer by drawer.

Dedicate yourself to preparing this place so the love of your life feels safe and happy and at home.

The love of your life is you.

Dedicate time to make notes and collect all your observations about how something makes you feel and why you'd want it in your space.

_____

_____

_____

_____

How about things you want to not have in your space?

_____

_____

_____

_____

How can you clear them out?

_____

_____

_____

_____

Learn something new.

What would you like to try your hand at?

Maybe you want to learn how to write better. Or paint. Or play a musical instrument. Or code.

Make this list and then make sure you come back to it and add to it.

Then, get busy checking it off.

You should always be learning something new.

Make a list of things you've always wanted to learn — extra points if you suspect you might never get good at them, because this is not about prowess. It's about pleasure. About joy.

_____

_____

_____

_____

Boundaries.

Boundaries are how we relate to others and how we build healthy relationships. They are self-esteem: they are how self-esteem shows itself.

I might say *"I've had a long day and I'm going to take a bath before I do anything else"* or *"I don't do any work on Saturdays"* or *"I don't want to talk about this right now."*

A boundary is me saying I respect myself. It's me saying I am going to stand up for what I need.

A boundary is me considering myself worth representing.

A relationship boundary is an expression of where your limits are, where you end and another person begins.

A relationship without boundaries does not feel healthy. I feel disloyal if I do anything that does not involve us, like wanting to spend time alone or with friends. I experience difficulty saying *"no"*, as if saying no were an act of betrayal or proof of my selfishness.

I confuse my own emotions with his, and step in to conduct how he is feeling and what he is doing with his time. I feel responsible if he is sad or lonely or frustrated, as if fixing things for him was my responsibility.

Your body has a built in signal for compromising too much, and it's called "resentment". It comes disguised as anger towards another person, but really you are angry at yourself for not setting clear boundaries.

Some examples of boundaries:

Do you mind if we make plans without the other on Sunday? I am feeling like I need time alone.

I know you're trying to support me but I am not ready to talk about that yet.

I understand you are angry, but it's not OK for you to slam the door.

I don't want to have sex tonight.

Please don't come visit me without letting me know first.

It's ok for us to not agree on this point but please don't force your perspective on me.

I cannot text you back immediately.

If I exercise boundaries, my relationships — instead of feeling increasingly more suffocating — have space. The people in the relationship are independent and know how to take care of themselves.

We both recognize we are not everything to the other: I cannot and should not be the person who meets every one of your needs.

We are comfortable misunderstanding the other, or arguing.

We are not one — we are two, and this is how we better love and support one another.

Meeting another person's expectations of you is impossible. If you tried you'd fall short forever, and in the process lose yourself.

Conversely, it's not another person's job to meet your expectations. Your expectations belong to you, and if you are hurt or disappointed because someone does not meet them, that is not on the other person but on you.

Are you clear on the concept of boundaries?

Do you experience difficulty saying no?

Are you worried about disappointing others?

Write about all of this.

A word about disappointing others:

I believe in what I'm going to call the disappointment imperative. I am completely ready and willing to disappoint anyone who wants something for me that I don't want for myself.

Write down examples of times when you have disappointed others.

_____

_____

_____

_____

Write down examples of times you worry you will disappoint others.

_____

_____

_____

_____

How does this impact your life?

_____

_____

_____

_____

> *Who lives with the consequences of these decisions?*

Create something.

The biggest, most beautiful manifestation of self-love is making time to create something.

I am a writer, so I write, but it can be anything. Pastries, companies, software, paintings, sculpture, delicious meals.

What are you creating? What do you want to create more of?

How can you give yourself the time?

A quick summary: your cheat sheet.

PART 1.

AS I GET TO KNOW MYSELF,
I DEVELOP FAITH IN ME.

FROM THIS,
I FEEL CALMER.
I SUFFER LESS.

PART 2.

I AM DRIVEN LESS BY WHAT MY E**GO** WANTS ME TO DO.

PART 3:
I AM MORE COMFORTABLE
IN THE MOMENT.

FROM THIS,
I APPROVE MYSELF.
I VALIDATE MYSELF.
I AM PROUD OF MYSELF.

I LOVE MYSELF.

Here is what we've worked on in this workbook. Here is what you have written about.

First, forever abandon the notion that self-care is selfish. This belief is destructive and ensures you end up isolated, resentful and depleted. This belief is why people burn out.

Ask yourself what you need. A bath? An orange? A divorce? What you need is hard to determine but the more you find time alone and the more patient you are with yourself the clearer the answer will become.

Consider learning how to meditate. It's the most glorious gift you will ever present yourself with: permission to set it all aside to make room for your breath.

Treat yourself like you would someone you love. With compassion, with generosity, with tolerance. *It's ok, Dushka. I've got you.*

Learn to say no. Boundaries are integral to this effort and saying no is a good start.

Make choices for you. If someone else tells you you are thinking of you instead of them, if they want to push you in a way that is to your detriment and their benefit — well, think about that.

Watch what you eat. Give yourself nutritious food.

Make sure you are sleeping well.

Learn how to breathe. Deep breaths change your life — they tell your body you are OK. Eventually breathing deeply pulls you out of feeling like life is something you have to survive.

Move. Exercise. Find something you like — or more than one thing — so it's less of an effort and more of a respite, a vacation, a reward.

Find pleasure. I will give you a tip: it's in your senses. Things that feel good, taste good, sound good. Beauty is primal and necessary. Surround yourself with it.

The meaning of life is in connection. Identify people who inspire you and build you up and keep them near you. A tip: these people are the ones who respect your boundaries.

Create something. A book. A garden. A dish. A company. We are creators.

There is solace and peace in repetition. Find your habits. Find your rituals. Find your ceremony. Serve yourself coffee every morning in silence. Pour it into a beautiful handmade cup. Write down things you are grateful for as you sip. Do it again, and again, and again.

Finally, these are not changes you make. This is a new life you step into. It's a practice, and you come back to it over and over. Did you say yes when you wanted to say no? It's ok. It's ok. You will try again tomorrow.

> *As you read this section, how did you feel?*
>
> *Is there anything you feel you need to review again, write again, do more research on, look up, rewrite, reconsider?*
>
> *Does your notebook need to be reviewed?*
>
> *Should you start another, and begin again?*
>
> *Loving yourself is a process. A practice. A new way to live.*
>
> *If you fill out this book once a year, every year will be different, a new stage in your own evolution.*
>
> *You will look back with wonder at how far you've come.*
>
> *You can always begin again.*

What happens as you learn to love yourself?

As I get to know myself, as I find my feet, as I slowly learn how to establish my boundaries and protect them, I develop faith.

I don't mean in religion — I mean in myself.

This kind of faith is a powerful antidote to anxiety.

Faith in myself is how I come to trust that things will work out.

From this, I feel calmer. I suffer less.

I am less driven by what my ego wants me to do. I can soothe her when she freaks out, when she spins out, instead of mistaking her for me.

I realize nothing is personal and that people are doing the best they can so it becomes much easier to forgive and let go of what once would have hurt me.

My relationships are deeper, more meaningful, more deliberate, more peaceful. There is less drama, less entitlement, less blame.

I feel respected and valued because I respect and value myself.

I am more comfortable in the moment, this one right in front of me, because I can see my stories (both about the past and about the future) and can separate myself from them.

I enjoy the frankly delightful pleasure of my own company.

It is very, very powerful to learn to do for myself all the things I expected I could extract from others — approve of myself, validate myself, and be proud. Proud of myself.

Go back to the first page of your notebook.

Read it. Get to know yourself.

Notice the progress you've made. How far you've come.

Be proud of you.

Love you.

Author's note:

I am so happy to have gone on this adventure within with you.

If you have questions about anything along the way, I suggest you enter my name and any key word — self-love, boundaries, resentment, rituals, breathing, meditation, ego, anything — on the Quora search window. This way you can find everything I've written about what you seek, and maybe come across other helpful things along the way.

Also, all my books expand on what I write about here. I particularly recommend my book about boundaries "How To Draw Your Boundaries and why no one else can help you", "Love Yourself and other insurgent acts that will recast everything", and "Feelings Are Fickle and other things I wish someone had told me".

I do want to underline that everything I write — including the content of the books I mention above — is available on Quora for free.

If you find any of this helpful, please write Amazon reviews so that other people who need it can find it too.

Dushka Zapata

San Francisco, California

March, 2021

About the Illustrator

Dan Roam is the author of five international bestselling books on visual storytelling. **The Back of the Napkin** was named by Fast Company, The London Times, and BusinessWeek as the "Creativity Book of the Year".

Dan is a creative director, author, painter, and model-builder. His purpose in life is to make complex things clear by drawing them and to help others do the same. Dan has helped leaders at Allbirds, Google, Microsoft, Boeing, Gap, IBM, the US Navy, and the Obama White House solve complex problems with simple pictures.

Dan and his whiteboard have appeared on CNN, MSNBC, ABC CBS, Fox, and NPR.

About the Author

Dushka Zapata has worked in communications for over twenty years, running agencies (such as Edelman and Ogilvy) and working with companies to develop their corporate strategy.

During this time she specialized in executive equity and media and presentation training. She helped people communicate better through key message refinement and consistency and coached them to smoothly manage difficult interviews with press during times of crisis.

Dushka is an executive coach and public speaker who imparts workshops about personal brand development. She has been hired for strategic alignment hiring, to coach and mentor high potential individuals, improve upon new business pitches, refine existing processes and galvanize a company's communication efforts.

She recently built and ran the communications team at Zendesk and is now head of communications for Forte, a start up that believes games can unlock new economic opportunities for billions of people.

Dushka is the author of eleven books: "How to be Ferociously Happy", "Amateur: an inexpert, inexperienced, unauthoritative, enamored view of life", "A Spectacular Catastrophe and other things I recommend", "Your Seat Cushion is a Flotation Device and other buoyant short stories", "Someone Destroyed My Rocket Ship and other havoc I have witnessed at the office", "How to Build a Pillow Fort and other valuable life lessons", "You Belong Everywhere and other things you'll have to see for yourself", "Love Yourself and other insurgent acts that recast everything", "Feelings Are Fickle and other things I wish someone had told me", "How to Draw Your Boundaries and why no one else can save you", and the one you have in your hands.

Dushka was recently named one of the top 25 innovators in her industry by The Holmes Report and regularly contributes to Quora, the question and answer site, where she has over 182 million views.

Printed in Great Britain
by Amazon